Patriotism

Recognizing Stereotypes

Patriotism

Recognizing Stereotypes

Curriculum Consultant: JoAnne Buggey, Ph.D.
College of Education, University of Minnesota

By Bonnie Szumski

Greenhaven Press, Inc.
Post Office Box 289009
San Diego, CA 92198-9009

Titles in the opposing viewpoints juniors series:

Smoking   Death Penalty
Gun Control   Drugs and Sports
Animal Rights   Toxic Wastes
AIDS   Patriotism
Alcohol   Working Mothers
Immigration   Poverty

Library of Congress Cataloging-in-Publication Data

Szumski, Bonnie, 1958-
　　Patriotism : recognizing stereotypes / curriculum consultant,
JoAnne Buggey : by Bonnie Szumski.
　　　p.　cm.
　　Summary: Various authors present opposing viewpoints on the
following questions: "What is patriotism?" "Is patriotism positive?"
and "Does America need a new patriotism?" Includes critical thinking
skills activities
　　ISBN 0-89908-640-3
　.　1. Patriotism—Juvenile literature. 2. Patriotism—United States—
Juvenile literature. 3. Critical thinking—Juvenile literature.
[1. Patriotism. 2. Critical thinking.]　I. Buggey, JoAnne.
II. Title.
　　JC329.S98　　1989
　　323.6'5—dc20　　　　　　　　　　　　　　　　89-37555
　　　　　　　　　　　　　　　　　　　　　　　　　　CIP
　　　　　　　　　　　　　　　　　　　　　　　　　　AC

Cover photo: Comstock, Inc.

ISBN: 0-89908-640-3

CONTENTS

An Introduction to Opposing Viewpoints

When people disagree, it is hard to figure out who is right. You may decide one person is right just because the person is your friend or relative. But this is not a very good reason to agree or disagree with someone. It is better if you try to understand why these people disagree. On what main points do they differ? Read or listen to each person's argument carefully. Separate the facts and opinions that each person presents. Finally, decide which argument best matches what you think. This process, examining an argument without emotion, is part of what critical thinking is all about.

This is not easy. Many things make it hard to understand and form opinions. People's values, ages, and experiences all influence the way they think. This is why learning to read and think critically is an invaluable skill. Opposing Viewpoints Juniors books will help

you learn and practice skills to improve your ability to read critically. By reading opposing views on an issue, you will become familiar with methods people use to attempt to convince you that their point of view is right. And you will learn to separate the authors' opinions from the facts they present.

Each Opposing Viewpoints Juniors book focuses on one critical thinking skill that will help you judge the views presented. Some of these skills are telling fact from opinion, recognizing propaganda techniques, and locating and analyzing the main idea. These skills will allow you to examine opposing viewpoints more easily.

Each viewpoint in this book is paraphrased from the original to make it easier to read. The viewpoints are placed in a running debate and are always placed with the pro view first.

Recognizing Stereotypes

In this Opposing Viewpoints Juniors book, you will be asked to identify and study stereotypes. Stereotypes are exaggerated descriptions of people or things. People who use stereotypes apply a general description to a whole group. They do not look at the individual characteristics of each member of the group. Stereotyping can be favorable. For example, saying that blacks are natural basketball players is using a stereotype, but a positive one. However, most stereotyping is negative. It is meant to make fun of or humiliate a person or group.

Stereotyping grows out of our prejudices, beliefs, or attitudes that we have about particular groups of people or things. When we stereotype people, we prejudge them. We assume that all people in a group have the same traits. For example, Mr. X thinks that all immigrants receive a "free ride" from the government. The Kaos, a family of Hmongs, happen to be his next-door neighbors. One Sunday afternoon, Mr. X notices that Mr. Kao has driven into his driveway in a brand new Toyota. While Mr. Kao's family admires the new car, Mr. X says to himself, "If it weren't for all that money they get from the government, they'd never be able to afford that new car." The idea that Mr. Kao's entire family may have pitched in to buy the car, or even that Mr. Kao may have taken out a bank loan to afford the car, never enters his mind. Why not? Because he has prejudged all immigrants and will keep his stereotype even if it is not true.

Stereotypes are often hard to recognize because they are fixed beliefs. People have held them for a long time. While many stereotypes are easy to identify—for instance, "poor people are lazy"—others may be less obvious. Learning to identify stereotypes can help you tell the difference between writers who use stereotypes to further their arguments and those who do not.

You can learn to identify stereotypes by asking yourself questions about a particular reading. If a writer is talking about a group of people or a thing that he or she dislikes, these questions may help you discover stereotypes: "What is being said about this group of people or this thing? Is this group or thing being labeled unfairly?"

We asked two students to give their opinion of patriotism. Look for stereotypes in their arguments.

Being patriotic means loving your country and supporting it

My family is very patriotic. Whenever we are at a sporting event, for instance, my whole family sings the "Star-Spangled Banner" really loud. It's kind of embarrassing, but sometimes my mom even cries when she hears the part about "the land of the free and the home of the brave."

One time, my dad noticed someone not standing up during the song. He went down to the man and said, "Aren't you proud to be an American?" The guy just laughed. My dad got so angry, he punched him. Even though my mom said he shouldn't have punched him, I think my dad is right. People like that take our country for granted. They think they can just make fun of our country and the flag.

I mean, why do people like that think all these immigrants come here? They come here because other countries kill and hurt their people. In other countries, people are scared and hungry all the time. Immigrants come to America because they know they can live like kings compared to the way they used to live.

Patriotism to me means being loyal. Our family doesn't make fun of the president or criticize him. We just know he has to know what's right. A president may make mistakes, but he knows a lot more than we do. People who criticize the president are unpatriotic.

Being patriotic means criticizing your country

I just hate people who say they are patriotic. They seem like they're afraid to say the U.S. isn't perfect. And it isn't. My dad says that a real patriot stands up for what he thinks our country *should* be, not what it is. He says people who call themselves patriots are really just cowards. They want to close their eyes to the problems in this country.

My grandfather, for instance, hates the Republicans. And I agree with him. The fact is, they're just money-grubbing rich people who don't care about the country. But they're the ones that always say how patriotic they are. What a joke!

Patriotism means criticizing your country and trying to make it better. If we didn't do that, we'd be just like Nazis—following along without thinking about what's wrong or right.

ANALYZING THE
SAMPLE VIEWPOINTS

Suzanne and Robert have very different opinions about patriotism. Both of them use examples of stereotyping in their arguments.

Suzanne:

STEREOTYPES

People who don't stand up for the flag are unpatriotic.

All immigrants come to America because of poverty and hunger.

People who criticize the president are unpatriotic.

Robert:

STEREOTYPES

A real patriot stands up for what he thinks.

Republicans are money-grubbing rich people.

People who don't criticize their country are Nazis.

In this sample, Suzanne and Robert use an equal number of stereotypes.

Both Suzanne and Robert think they are right about patriotism. What conclusions about patriotism would you come to from this sample? Why?

Can you think of other examples of stereotypes you have come across in your reading or that you have heard people use?

As you continue to read through the viewpoints in this book, watch out for examples of stereotyping. Remember to question whether an author is portraying a group unfairly.

CHAPTER 1

PREFACE: What Does Patriotism Mean?

One dictionary defines patriotism as a "love for or devotion to one's country." While there seems to be no disagreement that this is what patriotism means, many people disagree over what is the right way to love their country.

In the next two viewpoints, each author presents ideas about how people should love their country. The first author believes that patriotism means swearing loyalty to one's country whether it is right or wrong. The second author believes that true patriotism means improving the country, not pledging a blind loyalty to it.

When reading these two viewpoints, pay attention to the stereotypes the two authors use.

Patriotism means loyalty to one's country

Editor's Note: The following viewpoint is paraphrased from an article by Gary Bauer. Mr. Bauer worked for President Ronald Reagan. In this article, he argues that patriotism means being loyal to your country.

Even though it is a positive statement, the author is stereotyping all Americans.

What does the author think of "hippies?" This is a stereotype.

The author suggests that the Soviet people want to destroy our freedom. Are the Soviets being portrayed fairly? Or is the author stereotyping?

What is being said about the Soviets and the Americans in this paragraph? The author is stereotyping all Soviets and all Americans.

Every school child can quote the words from the "Star-Spangled Banner," "The land of the free and the home of the brave." These are words that inspire all Americans. Americans take pride in their independence and in their history. America is a country born in freedom and in God.

It is this love of liberty that makes our country unique. No other nation can claim as much dedication to freedom as America.

These attitudes keep America united but are under constant threat. In the 1960s and 1970s, young people called "hippies" burned the American flag and cursed America. Although this rarely happens, I am still uneasy. There are still too many people who think it is all right to criticize their country.

We must create in our children a feeling of pride about America. I am afraid that we are failing to do this.

I saw this when I read about some children from a gifted and talented class. These children had been taught to believe that there was no difference between Americans and the Soviets. In fact, one boy said that there are no "bad guys" in the world! This boy has no sense of what the world is like. He will grow up not understanding that there are men and women—especially Soviet men and women—in the world who hate America. These people and others would like nothing more than to destroy our freedom.

Another example I read about in the newspaper was about a gathering of Soviet and American children. The Soviet children helped the American children drape a "peace ribbon" around the Pentagon. The Soviet children told the American children that the Pentagon caused war and threatened peace. Something is terribly wrong when the sons and daughters of people who want to destroy freedom—the Soviets—try to teach freedom to Americans, who are truly free.

At first I am angry when I hear these stories, but then I realize these are just children. Children need us to teach them the truth. The world is not an innocent place. Other countries would like to destroy us. America is the one country that stands for freedom.

For love of liberty, Americans have gone to war. They have done this to preserve their freedom and the freedom of others. America has never waged war to profit or to conquer other countries. America's purpose has always been to preserve freedom and to help other countries gain it.

And why, if our country is so bad, do thousands of immigrants come here of their own free will? We should teach our children why the immigrants come. They come, fleeing their homelands, for a chance to raise their children in freedom. These people still risk death for a chance to live in our great country.

> Immigrants come to the U.S. for different reasons, such as jobs or family. The author is stereotyping immigrants.

We must teach our children about these things. We must teach them about the people who speak of America as a beacon of perfection—"a shining city upon a hill." We must also teach them about people who would gladly die for their country, such as the one who said, "Give me liberty or give me death." They should know our heroes and what the Statue of Liberty stands for. They should know what the Berlin Wall is and why it is there. Our children must love the things we love and preserve the things worth preserving.

> The author has a very positive view of what we should teach children about the U.S. Is he stereotyping the U.S.? Why or why not?

DEFENDER OF OUR FREEDOMS

© Germano/ROTHCO

Is America better than other countries?

State three of the reasons Mr. Bauer gives for believing the U.S. is better than other countries. Do you agree that America is the most honest, most free country in the world? Why or why not? Is Mr. Bauer using our emotions about our country in order to get us to agree with him? Why or why not?

Patriotism means criticizing one's country

Editor's Note: The following viewpoint is paraphrased from an article by Michael Parenti. Mr. Parenti is well known for criticizing U.S. involvement in other countries. He has also written many books. In this article, Mr. Parenti criticizes what he calls "superpatriots," or people who are completely loyal. True patriotism, he thinks, means trying to improve America.

Who are the superpatriots? Is the author stereotyping people who criticize him?

The author is arguing that superpatriots all believe the same thing. This is an example of stereotyping.

Whenever I criticize America, I am always asked, "But don't you love your country?" The people who ask me this question think that because I criticize my country, I am not patriotic. I call this kind of thinking "superpatriotism." By this I mean following your country and leaders uncritically and accepting everything your country does because it would be unpatriotic not to do so.

Superpatriotism is used a lot to try to stop people from criticizing their country. But what do superpatriots mean when they say they love their country? Do they mean they love America's history? I don't think so. For one thing, superpatriots seem to remember only the bits they want to remember. They don't seem to recognize the terrible side of American history—the mass killing of the Indians, slavery, and the wars against Spain, Central America, and Vietnam.

Superpatriots say they love America, but what they love is not really a place at all. Their America is a symbol. Their America consists of nothing but a flag and slogans like "My country, right or wrong." But superpatriots really just love war and the military. Usually, when they want to talk about the America they love, they talk about the wars and the battles we have fought.

Superpatriots' love for their country is based on competing with other countries. They say that if we really love our country, we have to say that it is better than all other countries. They want America to be "number one."

But what are we number one in? It seems to me that the only two things we are number one in are our wealth and our military strength. But the superpatriots don't care how the money is spent or where the military is used.

The superpatriots never explain why it is important to be number one. But I don't think it is very important. People who respect liberty, democracy, and equality should not be concerned with beating out other countries. They should be concerned with their own country.

Superpatriots don't *really* care about America. They care about being loyal to a symbol. They are loyal to a flag, or a song, or an image. This attitude is dangerous. What it asks us to think is that anything the nation does is O.K., that anything our leaders decide is necessary should be done. Even terrible violence is O.K. and even considered heroic if it is done to protect the nation.

When Americans first recognized the evil that was being done by our country during the Vietnam War, many attacked the symbols of patriotism. They burned American flags. These people were called unpatriotic by the military. But what is a real patriot?

Real patriots love their country. They love it so much that they want to improve it. Real patriots know that democracy is not just elections. Democracy is helping the welfare of everyone who lives in America. Real patriots do not just love other Americans, they love everyone in the world. They want America to treat other countries with respect.

Real patriots take pride in an American history that is different from the one the superpatriots brag about. They are proud of the abolition of slavery, the peace movement, the end of child labor, and the civil rights movement.

Real patriots want to love both their country and justice too. As real patriots, we should fight to eliminate poverty, even if it means asking the rich to pay more of their share. We should make companies clean up the environment so America will be more safe for everyone. We should want more job training for people who are out of work. We should want a national health insurance program so that no one goes without medical treatment.

America belongs to the people. True patriotism means taking our country back from the corporations and politicians. Let's stand together and improve our country.

Who are the people who respect liberty? The author is stereotyping real patriots.

Is the author's definition of real patriots a stereotype? Why or why not?

Can patriots criticize their country?

What kind of patriotism does Mr. Parenti criticize? Do you agree with his criticism? What is your definition of patriotism?

1

Recognizing Stereotypes

After reading the two viewpoints on the meaning of patriotism, make a chart similar to the one made for Suzanne and Robert on page 10. List the stereotypes each author uses to make his case. Remember that many of the stereotypes in these readings have already been pointed out to you. Take a few minutes to review the questions in the margins of the readings before making your list. A chart is started for you below:

Bauer:

STEREOTYPES

Something is terribly wrong when Soviet children—sons and daughters of people who hate freedom—teach freedom to the truly free.

Parenti:

STEREOTYPES

Superpatriots just love war and the military.

Which article used the most stereotypes? After reading the two articles, which did you think was the most convincing? Why? List some stereotypes besides the ones in the articles that you have heard about patriots.

PREFACE: **Is Patriotism Positive?**

Since the founding of America, the value of patriotism has been questioned. Two well-known quotations summarize the debate. Samuel Johnson, an English author, said in 1775, "Patriotism is the last refuge of a scoundrel." Stephen Decatur, an American naval officer, said in 1816, "Our country! In her intercourse with foreign nations, may she always be in the right; but our country, right or wrong." In both of these quotes, the issue is whether or not patriotic loyalty is positive. Samuel Johnson argues that patriotism is something to hide behind—to cover up deeds one may be ashamed of. Decatur believes the opposite; true loyalty demands standing behind your country even if it is wrong.

The next two viewpoints expand on this issue. In the first, Robert Heinlein argues that patriotism is positive. He believes that it is essential to human survival. John S. Spong, in the second viewpoint, holds the opposite opinion. He believes that unless we stop being loyal to a single nation, we are doomed.

As you read these viewpoints, pay close attention to whether the authors base their arguments on stereotypes.

Editor's Note: This viewpoint is paraphrased from an article by Robert Heinlein. Robert Heinlein was a well-known science fiction writer who died in 1988. Mr. Heinlein argues that patriotism is the most noble and practical of all human emotions.

The author criticizes the beliefs of a whole group of people who disagree with him. Is he stereotyping them?

What does the author say about people who would not defend themselves? Is this a stereotype? Why or why not?

" Want this wrapped or will you burn it here?"

© Uluschak/ROTHCO

In the United States, it is popular to make fun of patriotism. Especially so-called "intellectuals" (people who think they know everything) seem to think that every civilized person should hate war and disapprove of the military. "Warmongers," "imperialists," "hired guns in uniform"—you have all heard such remarks and you will hear them again. One of the "intellectuals'" favorite quotations is, "Patriotism is the last refuge of a scoundrel."

Patriotism is the most practical of all human emotions. It is what saves a country from destruction.

But now true patriots are often too shy to talk about it. I do not understand this. Patriotism is not something to be ashamed of. People must feel patriotism to survive.

Human beings are alive and must continue to stay alive. It makes sense, then, that the only emotions that human beings must have are ones that help the species survive. Patriotism helps human beings survive. To show you how, I have broken human behavior into four levels:

The first level is when a person or animal fights for his/her own survival. While this may seem selfish, it is important. Any living thing that will not fight for its own survival is doomed.

The second level is to work, fight, and sometimes die for your own family. When parents jump into the water to save a drowning child or take on a second job to help the children, they are putting the welfare of another family member above their own.

The third level is to work, fight, and sometimes die for a group larger than the family—a tribe, herd, or pack. This kind of behavior can be found in animals—especially baboons. Baboons will act to protect the entire tribe from harm and die doing it.

Patriotism is the fourth and highest level of behavior. When loyalty and duty are shown toward a group so large that your cannot personally know each of its members—this is patriotism.

This kind of behavior can be seen in the astronauts who risk their lives so that human beings can explore new planets.

Patriotism is as practical as making sure your car is in good working order. With patriotism, people admit that the survival of the nation is more important than their individual lives. Sailors at sea have four words to describe patriotism: "Women and children first." Patriotism ensures the survival of the species. A large percentage of the males of a species can die, but without women and children, human beings are headed the way of the dinosaurs.

And extinction is the way we are headed. Other nations have vanished; ours may, too.

No one can be forced to feel patriotism. We cannot have a patriotism law. We cannot buy it, no matter how much money we spend. The feeling of patriotism is something that comes from the inside. I want to tell you a story about one man from my hometown who had it.

On weekends, my family used to go to a park that had picnic benches, a zoo, and a lake. All the families in the town would go there. There was only one thing wrong with it: It was cut through the middle by railroad tracks. One day a young man and his wife were crossing the tracks when the woman caught her foot in the tracks.

The husband tried hard to get his wife's foot loose, but could not. A tramp walked up to the man and his wife and also started trying to get the young woman's foot out of the tracks. Just then, all three of them heard the train coming. The two men struggled to free the woman, right up until all three were hit by the oncoming train.

We can understand the husband's role. After all, it was his duty to save his wife. But what about the tramp? The tramp died to save a woman he did not even know. And that is the essence of patriotism.

This is how a human being is supposed to live...and die.

What is the author's definition of a true patriot? Is he stereotyping?

The author argues that anyone who is not willing to die for a stranger is unpatriotic.

What is patriotism?

What is Mr. Heinlein's definition of patriotism? Does it differ from the definitions of patriotism you have read elsewhere? If so, how? As you continue to read the viewpoints in this book, pay close attention to the different definitions of patriotism the authors present.

VIEWPOINT 4 Patriotism must die

Editor's Note: This viewpoint is paraphrased from the views of John S. Spong. Mr. Spong is an Episcopal bishop in New Jersey. In this viewpoint, he argues that patriotism is destructive and must be eliminated.

The author characterizes all early people as being unable to view themselves as individuals. Is this an example of stereotyping? Why or why not?

In the twentieth century, patriotism is no longer necessary. In fact, patriotism is so harmful to society that it must be destroyed. These may seem like harsh words, and some people may react strongly against them. But patriotism divides the world into "us" and "them." We can no longer afford to do this. Where once patriotism bound our nation together, it now must be rejected.

Life was hard and dangerous for early human beings. People's lives were constantly threatened by wild animals, sickness, and death. Early people could not think of themselves as individuals. Individual people's lives were too fragile, and death came too easily. In that time, everyone had to work for the good of the whole to survive. Loyalty to the tribe was a necessity, and this was the beginning of the emotion that we call patriotism. The tribe was supposed to protect the interests of the group and to defend itself against other tribes.

Eventually, these tribes became nations. To this day, it would be hard to think of ourselves as not part of a nation. Our citizenship to a particular nation is a large part of our personal identity. It is hard to imagine a world without nations, but it is coming. It has to.

Slowly, the need for separate nations is dying. Technology, especially, is responsible. Television has brought war, famine, and other tragedies around the world to our attention. We now see how linked we are to other countries in the world. Businesses, too, because of air travel, have become more international. All of these changes have made us realize that we are part of a community of nations. We can no longer think that our nation is the best.

The final blow to patriotism and separate nations will come when we realize the environmental dangers that face us all. All human beings must drink the earth's water, eat food from the earth's oceans, and breathe air from the earth's atmosphere. A polluted river in the Soviet Union, a nuclear accident in Pennsylvania, or an oil spill off the coast of Australia affects the whole world. Individual nations cannot protect themselves from these dangers. It will take worldwide cooperation to ensure the survival of the planet.

This means that nations are losing their purpose. And when something loses its purpose, it dies out. While it may take a long time, nations' needs will start to lose importance and worldwide needs will take over.

All wars have been fought to ensure the survival of one particular nation or group of nations. There is no one enemy when pollution is destroying the planet on which all of us live. Thus my future is linked to that of people all over the world. It is no longer just one American's future.

Patriotism is an emotion that was essential when humans lived in tribes, but now it must die. We need to recognize human interdependence.

What will happen to begin this transformation? I believe a worldwide environmental disaster will cause nations to work together. While it is depressing to think that only a great tragedy will cause patriotism to die, it is perhaps the only way.

Why does the author believe the end of nations is here? Why does he believe we can no longer think our nation is best?

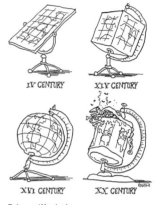

Palomo (Mexico)
© 1989 Cartoonists and Writers Syndicate

The author is not using stereotyping in this paragraph. But he is suggesting that people will start viewing themselves in a new way. What way is that?

Will patriotism die out?

Mr. Spong thinks that patriotism is no longer needed. Name two reasons he believes this. Do you agree with Mr. Spong that patriotism is no longer necessary? Why or why not?

Recognizing Stereotypes in Statements

Below is a list of statements related to patriotism. Consider each statement carefully. Mark S for any statement that is an example of stereotyping. Mark N for any statement that is not an example of stereotyping. Mark U if you are undecided about any statement. Then give a brief explanation of why you decided on your answer.

EXAMPLE: College students are unpatriotic.

ANSWER: S. Stereotype. Judging all college graduates as unpatriotic is an unfair generalization.

1. Every American must make his/her own decision about what patriotism means.

   Answer _____ Explanation _____

   _____

2. Kids today don't respect anything. They don't care about their country.

   Answer _____ Explanation _____

   _____

3. Immigrants are the most patriotic Americans. That's because they realize how great America is.

   Answer _____ Explanation _____

   _____

4. Some people believe anyone who criticizes his/her country is unpatriotic.

   Answer _____ Explanation _____

   _____

5. Politicians say that they are patriots just to get elected. They don't really care about the U.S.

   Answer _____ Explanation _____

   _____

PREFACE: **Does America Need a New Patriotism?**

In the next two viewpoints, the authors both have the same definition of what it meant to be patriotic in the past. But they disagree on what patriotism should mean today.

In the first viewpoint, Max Rafferty argues that Americans should return to the attitudes of the past. He believes American schoolchildren should be taught to revere patriotic heroes, such as George Washington and Nathan Hale. He also believes they should be taught to respect the military and the government. He argues that teachers have harmed America by not teaching students to take pride in its accomplishments.

In the second viewpoint, Ralph Nader argues that this type of patriotism must be rejected and a new patriotism must be found. He says that the new patriotism must be dedicated to making America better. This includes protecting the environment, helping poor people, and keeping a close watch on government.

As you read these two viewpoints, watch for stereotypes.

Editor's Note: This viewpoint is paraphrased from a speech by Max Rafferty. Max Rafferty is a Distinguished Professor at Troy State University in Alabama. He was awarded the George Washington Honor Medal by the Freedom Foundation at Valley Forge. In this viewpoint, Mr. Rafferty argues that Americans must return to the patriotism of colonial times.

There are very few patriots left in America. The reason is America's schools. All teachers, including myself, are responsible for this problem.

First, let us go back to a time of true patriotism. A young man is captured, questioned, tried as a spy, and convicted. He is surrounded by jeering enemies, beyond rescue. A rope is already knotted around his neck. He breaks the silence with one short sentence. His words come down to us today, ringing pure and true: "I only regret that I have but one life to lose for my country."

This man's statue stands today, gazing with blind stone eyes across a green park in New York City. The man, Nathan Hale, was a schoolmaster, and he did not live to see his twenty-second birthday.

FLAG DAY

What happened? I'm still the same old flag. Oh, I have a few more stars since you were a boy. Alot more blood has been shed since those parades of long ago.

But now I don't feel as proud as I use to. When I come down the street you just stand there with your hands in your pockets and I may get a small glance and then you look away. Then I see the children running around and shouting... they don't seem to know who I am... I saw one man take off his hat then look around, he didn't see anybody else with theirs off so he quickly put his back on.

Is it a sin to be patriotic anymore? Have you forgotten what I stand for? Where I've been? Anzio, Guadalcanal, Korea, Vietnam. Take a look at the Memorial Honor Rolls sometime, of those who never came back. All to keep this Republic free... One Nation Under God. When you salute me you are actually saluting them.
Well it won't be long before I'm coming down your street again. So, when you see me stand straight, place your right hand over your heart. And I'll salute you, by waving back.'
Anon

Dobbins, *Manchester Union Leader.* Reprinted by permission.

What would those stone eyes make of young men and women today who seem to spend every minute criticizing our country? What would those stone eyes think of these young people who despise and boo Congress?

Whether we like it or not, the reason our children criticize our country so much is because of today's teachers.

These children are now adults, a group of spineless, luxury-loving, spiritless characters. They came right out of America's classrooms. They played in our kindergartens. They went on field trips to the bakery. They studied things called "sociology" and "arts" in our junior high schools. They were taught that competition was bad. They were told little about democracy. They were taught that the world was to become one big, happy family. They were taught to be kind and democratic and peaceful.

These last goals seem positive. What went wrong?

There were two things that we *did not* teach them. And oh, how they need to learn these!

One was that most of the people on this planet hate Americans. This is hard to teach, but it is a simple truth. The other, which would have been simpler, is the meaning of Decatur's toast, "Our country, right or wrong!"

Had they been taught these things, they would know that their country is in danger, and that would be enough. It was enough in 1898, and 1917, and 1941. It is not enough today. Too many of them neither know nor care.

It is our own fault. What will history have to say of the teachers of the 1930s, 1940s, and 1950s? We forgot that the first duty of a nation's schools is to preserve the nation.

We allowed words that America treasured to fade from the classroom. "Liberty and Union, now and forever, one and inseparable." "We have met the enemy and they are ours."

Search for these phrases today, and you will not find them. We have no further need of Daniel Websters or of Nathan Hales.

What does the author think of young people today? Is this a stereotype? Why or why not?

What is being said about most people on the planet? Is it fair?

Whom does the author believe students are asked to admire today? Is this a stereotype of education? What heroes have you been taught about?

But we also forgot something else. Patriotism needs hero-worship, and we eliminated heroes. Even the fairy tales and nursery rhymes children have loved for ages are now thought to be too violent and brutal. Everything that was scary and wonderful we made boring and average. Our textbooks are crowded with adventures of Tommy and Sue going on trips to the zoo, to the dump, or to the bakery. But the ride of Paul Revere goes unhonored and unsung. Education has eliminated the hero to make room for the jerk.

Today's hero—if there is one—is made in the image of ourselves.

He is daddy or mommy coming home from work. He is the postman on his route. He is the doctor at the hospital. He is all of the ordinary, boring people that populate our elementary textbooks. When I think of the doors we have closed upon the children! The great parade of heroes who made earth a magic place for boys and girls! Robin Hood and Ivanhoe and King Arthur—were not these fit heroes for children?

Most schools on all levels are teaching meaningless things about meaningless people. If you think I am lying, visit classroom after classroom, as I have done.

© Punch/Rothco

Watch the smart children become bored as they yawn over Bill and Tom's Trip to the Farm, or Sally's Fun at the Orange Grove. Then, suddenly, give them the story of the wrath of Achilles. Trek with them in spirit to the Yukon and, with brave Buck, let them answer *The Call of the Wild*. Let them thrill to those words flashing out of our past, "I have not yet begun to fight." Kneel with them behind the cotton bales at New Orleans with Andy Jackson at their side, as the redcoats begin to emerge from the Louisiana mists.

Watch their faces. See their eyes brighten and revive. They dream, they live, they glow. Patriotism will come easily to them, as it does to all of us who know our nation's past—and love it.

We must teach our children the importance of patriotism. We want our children to be in love with our country. We want them to oppose the communist menace.

If we start to teach our children right, our nation will again be a fit place for heroes.

How does the author characterize the "smart children?" Is this a stereotype? Why or why not?

What does the author believe is the only right way to teach our children? Do you think there is one right way?

Are children unpatriotic?

State two reasons the author gives to explain why children today are unpatriotic. Do you agree with the author's criticism that children do not have any heroes? Who are some of your heroes?

Editor's Note: This viewpoint is paraphrased from articles by Ralph Nader. Mr. Nader is a fighter for consumer rights. He is a lawyer and the author of many books. In this viewpoint, Mr. Nader says that America needs to abandon the patriotism of the past for a new patriotism.

Do you think there are only two ways to think about patriotism? Is the author stereotyping?

I was at a PTA meeting where people were talking about how many young people are fighting for civil rights and environmental issues. One woman stood up and asked, "But how can we teach children to be patriotic?"

This woman's question illustrates a point of view that helps us understand the debate over patriotism. On one side people believe that questioning people in authority like presidents, teachers, parents, and the government is wrong. They believe it is unpatriotic. On the other side are people who believe you can criticize the country and not be unpatriotic. I think it is time to talk about patriotism in a different way. I believe the meaning of patriotism can be found in the words, "liberty and justice for all."

© Garland/ROTHCO

In order to give patriotism a new meaning, we must look at four things. First, patriotism must come from an individual's beliefs and conscience. We have to know that our leaders in the White House and in the states are not perfect. When we think they are right, we should support them. But when we think they are wrong, we should criticize them, maybe even remove them from power. America is not its leaders. America is the people.

If we find our leaders using the military for immoral reasons, as they did in Vietnam, we must not support them. The flag, our country's symbol, must stand for liberty and justice. When we invade other countries, it stands for shame.

Second, patriotism starts at home. America must work to end poverty, racism, greed, and injustice.

Third, what is truly unpatriotic? Some people believe it is unpatriotic to tear down the flag. But I think it is more unpatriotic for corporations to pollute our land with toxic wastes. It is also unpatriotic to allow poverty to exist in our country. Our country's ideals must be upheld.

Fourth, patriotism should not be associated with wars and missiles. Patriots should be devoted to the concept of "I am my brother's keeper." Only when we protect the rights of every American are we being patriots.

My parents immigrated to the U.S. in 1912. My father was fond of saying that he took his freedom seriously. He meant that he wanted to participate in democracy. He wanted to work toward justice and a better society.

In the 1980s, patriotism is commercialized. Politicians use patriotism to get elected. The founding fathers, especially Washington and Lincoln, are used to advertise products. A schoolteacher friend of mine claims that when she holds up a picture of George Washington in front of preschoolers, they tell her that he's the one who sells cars.

What does the author argue the U.S. flag stands for? Is he stereotyping? Why or why not?

What does the author believe patriots should be devoted to? Is this a stereotype? Can you think of exceptions?

If you had to answer the author's question, how many children do you think know of our founding fathers? When did you first learn about Lincoln and Washington? Is the author's criticism fair, or is it an example of stereotyping?

This commercialization has little to do with patriotism. The corporations and media have taken over these symbols of pride. How many children know the history of the Statue of Liberty? How many children know the history of our founding fathers?

For me, the meaning of patriotism lies in making our country better. Loving America means protecting our environment. It means improving our roads and national parks.

Of course we have a government of the RICH. You don't expect us to waste government on the poor, do you?

© Carol*Simpson/Rothco

Loving America means helping its people. It means making sure little Americans are well fed and well educated. It means job training. It means loans to students. We should build a new, living patriotism.

We need a new patriotism that American citizens themselves must build. Citizens must unite to make America a better place to live.

Does patriotism mean making the U.S. better?

What is Mr. Nader's definition of a patriot? Do you agree?

Understanding Editorial Cartoons

Throughout this book, you have seen cartoons that illustrate the ideas in the viewpoints. Editorial cartoons are a usually humorous way of presenting an opinion on an issue. While many cartoons are easy to understand, others require more thought.

The cartoon below is similar to cartoons that appear in your daily newspaper. It deals with a subject that has come up frequently in this book—the meaning of patriotism. Examine the cartoon below and answer the questions that follow.

"It was designed as a flag, Buddy—not as a blindfold."

Why is the person hidden under the flag? Why do the words "obedience is patriotism" appear on the flag? What does the other person in the cartoon think of the person under the flag? How can you tell? What do you think the cartoonist's definition of patriotism would be? Why?

Do you think the cartoonist is stereotyping any particular group of people? Why or why not?